RSTONES
EEDOM™

GUN CONTROL

BY STEVEN OTFINOSKI

CHILDREN'S PRESS®
An Imprint of Scholastic Inc.
New York   Toronto   London   Auckland   Sydney
Mexico City   New Delhi   Hong Kong
Danbury, Connecticut

BRINGING HISTORY to LIFE

Content Consultant
James Marten, PhD
Professor and Chair, History Department
Marquette University
Milwaukee, Wisconsin

Library of Congress Cataloging-in-Publication Data
Otfinoski, Steven.
 Gun control / by Steven Otfinoski.
 pages cm. — (Cornerstones of freedom)
 Includes bibliographical references and index.
 Audience: Grade 4 to 6.
 ISBN 978-0-531-21331-5 (lib. bdg.) — ISBN 978-0-531-25827-9 (pbk.)
 1. Gun control—United States—Juvenile literature. I. Title.
 HV7436.O9185 2014
 363.33—dc23   2013022074

All rights reserved. Published in 2014 by Children's Press, an imprint of
Scholastic Inc.
Printed in the United States of America 113

SCHOLASTIC, CHILDREN'S PRESS, CORNERSTONES OF FREEDOM™,
and associated logos are trademarks and/or registered trademarks of
Scholastic Inc.

1 2 3 4 5 6 7 8 9 10 R 23 22 21 20 19 18 17 16 15 14

Photographs ©: Alamy Images: 22 (DIZ Muenchen GmbH, Sueddeutsche
Zeitung Photo), 11 (Stock Montage, Inc.), 23 (Stocktrek Images, Inc.),
41 (Texas Stock Photo), cover (YAY Media AS); AP Images: 28, 58
(Bob Jackson, Dallas Times-Herald), 2, 3, 47 (Brennan Linsley), 40
(David Longstreath), 45, 57 (Evan Vucci), 33 (John Hanna), 50 (Johnny
Hanson, Houston Chronicle), 38 (L.A. County Sheriff's Dept.), 8, 10, 12, 19
(North Wind Picture Archives), 51, 56 top (Ric Feld), 34 (Ron Edmonds),
48 (Steve Ueckert), 46 (Tom Uhlman); Corbis Images/Bettmann: 32; Getty
Images: 31 (Andrew Sacks), 35, 56 bottom (Chip Somodevilla), 5 bottom,
43 (David Handschuh/NY Daily News Archive), 20 (A. Dagli Orti/DEA), 36
(Dirck Halstead/Time Life Pictures), 4 top, 25 (Hedrich Blessing Collection/
Chicago History Museum), 44 (Jefferson County Sheriff's Department), 7
(Kateleen Foy), 26 (Roger Viollet), 6 (Spencer Platt); iStockphoto/
cbenjasuwan: back cover; Library of Congress: 24 (National Photo Company
Collection), 13, 16, 18; Media Bakery/Chase Swift: 55; Shutterstock, Inc./
mashurov: 4 bottom, 42; Superstock, Inc.: 14; The Advertising Archives:
5 top, 27; The Image Works: 17, 54 (Melanie Stetson Freeman/ Christian
Science Monitor), 49 (Monika Graff), 15 (North Wind Picture Archives),
30 (TopFoto).

Maps by XNR Productions, Inc.

Did you know that studying history can be fun?

BRING HISTORY TO LIFE by becoming a history investigator. Examine the evidence (primary and secondary source materials); cross-examine the people and witnesses. Take a look at what was happening at the time—but be careful! What happened years ago might suddenly become incredibly interesting and change the way you think!

Contents

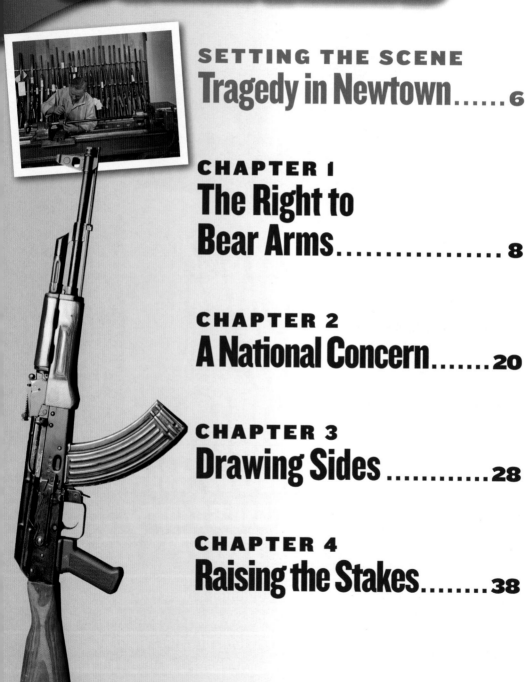

Tragedy in Newtown

Newtown, Connecticut, residents marked the six-month anniversary of the Sandy Hook shootings with an event honoring the victims who died in the attack.

December 14, 2012, began as just another school day at Sandy Hook Elementary School in the quiet suburban community of Newtown, Connecticut. But at about

9:30 a.m., 20-year-old Adam Lanza arrived. He entered the school carrying three weapons, including a **semiautomatic** Bushmaster rifle. What happened next was unimaginable.

Lanza moved through the school, firing at the students and teachers inside. Police found a horrific scene when they arrived less than 15 minutes later. Twenty students and six school employees lay dead. Lanza had taken his own life.

News of the shootings sent shock waves throughout the nation. Many people called for stricter gun laws to prevent future tragedies. At the same time, others argued that such laws would only be an inconvenience for law-abiding Americans who wanted to buy guns. The Newtown tragedy reignited the debate over one of the nation's most controversial issues—gun control.

Shooter Adam Lanza used guns belonging to his mother in his attack on Sandy Hook Elementary School.

RATE OF GUN OWNERSHIP IN THE WORLD.

CHAPTER 1

THE RIGHT TO BEAR ARMS

Guns have played an important role in American history since the arrival of the first European settlers.

GUN CONTROL REFERS TO THE limiting and restricting of citizens to buy, possess, and use firearms. This topic was not a major issue during most of the first two centuries of U.S. history. When the first European settlers arrived in North America in the early 1600s, guns were needed for survival. Colonists used **muskets** and pistols to hunt for food. They also used the guns to protect themselves from wild animals and in their conflicts with Native Americans and rival colonists from other European nations.

Colonial militiamen fought alongside trained British soldiers in the French and Indian War (1754–1763).

Firearms were so important to life in the American wilderness that some colonies made it a legal requirement that their citizens have working guns. In 1770, the colony of Georgia even passed a law that required all citizens to take their guns to church with them.

The Creation of Militias

In Europe, most nations had standing armies made up of professional soldiers. These armies protected the nation and its people in times of war. The North American colonies had no resources for a standing army. They relied instead on **militias**. These military groups were made up of ordinary citizens who came together in times of trouble. White males between the ages of 16 and 60 were required by law to serve in militias, and most brought their own firearms with them. Some colonial towns and cities had arms and ammunition that they stored in **arsenals**. These militias played an important role in various colonial wars of the 17th and 18th centuries. For example, a New England militia defeated an alliance of Native Americans during King Philip's War (1675–1676) without assistance from the British military.

An estimated 600 colonists and 3,000 Native Americans died during King Philip's War.

By the 1760s, more British soldiers were being sent to keep order in the colonies and to enforce laws. Many colonists didn't like having these soldiers among them. They also believed that the taxes Britain was placing on them were unfair. In some cases, the British government forced colonists to feed and house British soldiers who had no barracks to live in. All this supported a negative view of standing armies among the colonists.

The Revolution

Tension between Great Britain and the colonies grew in the 1770s. In April 1775, British general Thomas Gage led a force to Concord, Massachusetts, to destroy colonial militia supplies that were stored there. Militiamen met

Many of the colonists who fought in the American Revolution were citizens who used their personal firearms to battle the more professional British soldiers.

After leading the colonists to victory in the American Revolution, General George Washington (on horseback) was chosen to be the nation's first president.

the troops at the towns of Lexington and Concord, and drove them back. It was the beginning of the American Revolution. Colonial militiamen continued to play a prominent role in the war.

Not everyone at the time of the American Revolution thought militias were the best line of defense against the British troops. General George Washington led the Continental army, which was made up of professional soldiers. He said that local militias were "incapable of making or sustaining a serious attack."

Fifty-five representatives from the individual states participated in the 1787 Constitutional Convention.

The Bill of Rights

The war finally ended with America's independence from Great Britain in 1783. The 13 colonies were now a new nation called the United States of America. Each colony became a separate state within the country. Representatives of 12 of the 13 states met in Philadelphia, Pennsylvania, in the summer of 1787 to write a **constitution** for the United States. The constitution created a strong, central federal government. However, the individual states also had the power to make their own laws.

Some representatives were concerned that the new constitution did not address the rights of individual citizens. They called for 10 **amendments** that would legally guarantee such rights. James Madison of Virginia was the main writer of these amendments. Together, they were known as the Bill of Rights. The Bill of Rights' Second Amendment addressed the need for a well-armed militia. It reads: "A well-regulated militia, being necessary to the security of a free state, the right of the people to keep and bear arms, shall not be infringed [violated]." The wording of this amendment has caused much of the controversy over gun control. Some people believe that Madison and the other founders meant that only state militias have the right to bear arms. Others believe that the right is granted to individual citizens as well.

James Madison, the primary author of the Bill of Rights, was elected the fourth president of the United States in 1808.

A FIRSTHAND LOOK AT
THE VIRGINIA DECLARATION OF RIGHTS

James Madison's Second Amendment to the Constitution was influenced by the wording of similar amendments to state constitutions. Among these was the Virginia Declaration of Rights, which states, "That a well-regulated militia, composed of the body of the people, trained to arms, is the proper, natural, and safe defense of a free state." See page 60 for a link to read the entire declaration online.

Changing Guns for a Changing Time

In the 1800s, more Americans began moving westward in search of land and opportunities. The West was untamed. It contained many dangers, and guns were

Many settlers traveled westward across the United States in covered wagons during the 1800s.

necessary for survival. Back East, new and better ways to make guns were being discovered. Inventor Eli Whitney opened a musket factory in 1798 near New Haven, Connecticut. Previously, craftsmen had made guns by hand. Every gun was unique. If a part broke, it could not be replaced. Workers in Whitney's factory assembled guns using standard parts. This meant that the same parts used in one gun could also be used in another. This process made guns cheaper to make and easier to repair.

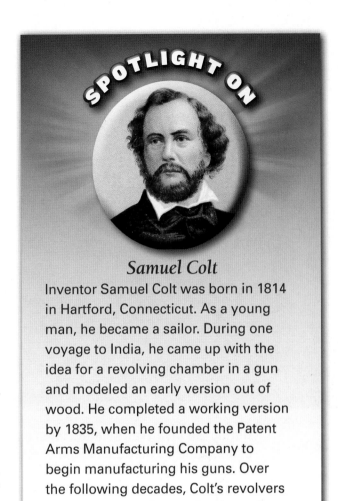

SPOTLIGHT ON

Samuel Colt

Inventor Samuel Colt was born in 1814 in Hartford, Connecticut. As a young man, he became a sailor. During one voyage to India, he came up with the idea for a revolving chamber in a gun and modeled an early version out of wood. He completed a working version by 1835, when he founded the Patent Arms Manufacturing Company to begin manufacturing his guns. Over the following decades, Colt's revolvers became extremely popular throughout America, and Colt continued to make improvements to his design.

In the 1830s, an inventor named Samuel Colt built a handgun with a revolving chamber. This allowed the gun to hold up to six bullets at a time. Previous guns had to be reloaded each time they were fired. The Colt revolver quickly became a standard weapon for lawmen and criminals alike. It came to be known as the "gun that won the West."

During the Civil War, soldiers often mounted bayonets on the ends of their guns so they could fight in close combat when needed.

The Union army bought thousands of firearms to fight the Confederates during the Civil War (1861–1865). After the war, more Americans moved to the West. They took their Colt revolvers and other firearms with them.

Though the Union soldiers had used guns during the Civil War, most of them were poor marksmen. This was seen as a problem by military officers even after the war ended. Two Union officers, Colonel William Church and General George Wingate, founded the National Rifle Association (NRA) in 1871 to improve the shooting skills of soldiers and civilians alike. They bought a farm on Long Island, New York, where they held shooting competitions. In the early 20th century, the NRA established rifle clubs at colleges and military academies across the country. It also set up numerous youth programs.

By the start of the 20th century, most of the United States was settled and developed. People living in towns and cities did not need guns to hunt for food or defend themselves. Police departments had been formed to combat crime. The need to bear arms seemed less important. But if there was less of a need for guns, did that mean there would also be little need to control the use of them?

YESTERDAY'S HEADLINES

Today, many people imagine the Wild West of movies and novels when they think about the history of westward expansion. However, many western towns actually had strict laws about firearms. Lawmen often required visitors to hand over their guns upon entering the town limits. Additionally, the citizens of many western towns were in favor of more gun control in their streets. Here is an editorial from the *Dodge City Times* of Dodge City, Kansas, published on July 12, 1883:

> There is a disposition [feeling] to do away with the carrying of firearms, and we hope the feeling will become general. The carrying of firearms is a barbarous [uncivilized] custom, and it's time the practice was broken up.

CHAPTER 2

A NATIONAL CONCERN

President William McKinley (front left) was assassinated by Leon Czolgosz (with gun). McKinley's vice president, Theodore Roosevelt, succeeded him as president.

ON SEPTEMBER 6, 1901, President William McKinley held a public reception at the Pan-American Exposition in Buffalo, New York. A long line of citizens waited to shake the president's hand at the exposition's Temple of Music. Among them was Leon Czolgosz, an **anarchist**. As McKinley reached out for Czolgosz's hand, Czolgosz shot him twice with a revolver. McKinley died of his wounds about a week later. He was the third U.S. president to be assassinated. It was an ominous beginning to a century that would be filled with gun violence.

Submachine guns, like the one carried by the man on the right, were popular with criminals and law enforcers alike during the 1920s.

The Roaring Twenties

By the 1920s, gun violence had reached a new level in the United States. In 1919, the alcohol trade had been outlawed. This led to groups of gangsters battling to control the illegal trade of alcohol. They fought openly in the streets of American cities. Newly invented firearms such as the submachine gun were the weapons of choice for many gangsters. This automatic gun could fire up to 800 bullets per minute.

Some states had gun control laws by the 1920s, but there were no national laws to control the selling and buying of guns. The escalating violence caused by powerful new guns led the American public to call for national gun laws. The first of these laws was the Miller Act of 1927. The Miller Act banned the delivery of handguns through the U.S. mail. Some gun owners opposed the new law. They argued that it was a violation of the Second Amendment. The law finally passed, but quickly proved ineffective. Gun sellers got around it by shipping their guns to customers using private carrier services.

SPOTLIGHT ON

The Thompson Machine Gun

The Thompson machine gun was one of the most popular weapons among early 20th-century gangsters. They called it the chopper, the Chicago piano, and the Tommy gun. This last nickname came from the gun's inventor, John Taliaferro Thompson. Thompson was a brigadier general in the U.S. Army. After serving in World War I (1914–1918), he invented his automatic gun with the help of his son, Marcellus. There were already automatic machine guns that could fire many rounds without being reloaded. However, they were very large and heavy. The submachine gun was lighter and more portable. Thompson meant his gun to be used as a military weapon. However, it became an ideal weapon for 1920s gangsters such as John Dillinger and George "Machine Gun" Kelly.

YESTERDAY'S HEADLINES

The Miller Act, which banned mail delivery of handguns, had many opponents. One of the most vocal was Texas congressman Thomas Blanton (above). During a 1924 congressional debate, he stated, "I do not believe this bill would stop a single thug or a single bootlegger [seller of illegal alcohol] or a single murderer from carrying firearms unlawfully."

Blanton's argument was based on the belief that criminals would continue to get their firearms illegally even if gun control laws were passed. This opinion is still voiced by people who oppose gun control today.

New Laws to Control Guns

As lawlessness grew in American cities, so did the public cry for more gun control. In 1934, Congress passed the National Firearms Act. The act required makers and sellers of guns to pay a tax for each weapon sold. It also required them to register the weapons and keep records of to whom they were sold. Buyers of these weapons had to pay a tax as well, and be fingerprinted before the gun sale could be completed. Other weapons, including bombs and grenades, could no longer be purchased by private citizens.

The Federal Firearms Act of 1938 took gun control a step farther. It required gun manufacturers and sellers to

Before the first gun laws were passed, anyone who wanted a gun could simply purchase one at a local store with no questions asked.

obtain a federal firearms license to ship any guns outside of their home states. It also stated that sellers could not sell guns to **felons**.

A FIRSTHAND LOOK AT
THE FEDERAL FIREARMS ACT OF 1938

The Federal Firearms Act was a major piece of gun control legislation signed by President Franklin D. Roosevelt on June 30, 1938. See page 60 for a link to read the act online.

A Supreme Court Decision

While many Americans supported these federal gun laws, many others were opposed to them. They believed that the new laws violated the Second Amendment. In 1939, two men were arrested for carrying an unregistered sawed-off shotgun across state lines from Oklahoma to Arkansas. While law enforcers claimed they had violated the National Firearms Act, the two

Many of the millions of U.S. soldiers who fought in World War II returned home with a desire to purchase guns of their own.

Guns were once commonly advertised as gifts for young boys.

Give him year 'round fun...for years to come

A Winchester 22 is a gift that keeps giving pleasure through the entire year. Built of better materials, to better designs, Winchester 22's deliver perfect service and flawless accuracy through years of hard use. So give your boy a Winchester, but more — give him the pleasure of your companionship. Take him shooting and take along your Winchester, too. Winchester 22's are priced from $17.95. Available in 10 models and 26 styles.

Prices subject to change without notice.

MODEL 61 — Straight line loading and precision rifling give target rifle accuracy. Shoots short, long or long rifle cartridges interchangeably. Price – $59.95.

MODEL 77 — A low-cost, self-loading 22 available in clip or tubular magazine. Smooth receiver — low scope mounting, fast rate of fire and high accuracy. Clip $46.95, tubular $52.25.

WINCHESTER
TRADEMARK

SPRING— Great time for plinking— tin cans, wood blocks — be sure to have a safe backstop when you shoot.

SUMMER — Take along a 22 rifle and plenty of Winchester or Western 22 ammunition to make picnics more fun.

FALL — Test your shooting skill on elusive, hard-to-hit squirrels. Check local game laws first.

WINTER— When you think you're really good, start stopping running rabbits with your 22 – tough, but fun.

WINCHESTER-WESTERN DIVISION • OLIN MATHIESON CHEMICAL CORPORATION • NEW HAVEN 4, CONNECTICUT

men claimed the law was unconstitutional. The case went to the Supreme Court, which ruled against the two men. The ruling stated that the Second Amendment referred only to weapons used by state militias and that a sawed-off shotgun had no "reasonable relationship to the preservation or efficiency of a well-regulated militia."

Just a few years after this ruling, World War II (1939–1945) ended in victory for the United States and its allies. American soldiers returned home with a new interest and enthusiasm for firearms. Gun sales soared as millions of Americans bought guns for hunting, marksmanship, and home protection. However, a shocking moment of gun violence soon changed many Americans' attitudes toward firearms.

CHAPTER 3

DRAWING SIDES

Lee Harvey Oswald was shot as police officers transferred him from a jail cell to an interrogation room.

At 12:30 p.m. on November 22, 1963, President John F. Kennedy was riding through Dallas, Texas, in a convertible limousine. Suddenly, shots rang out as the president's car passed through Dealey Plaza. Kennedy was shot twice, and he died within minutes. His assassin was a man named Lee Harvey Oswald. Oswald had killed the president using an Italian rifle he had purchased for $12.78 from a mail-order catalog. Two days after his arrest, Oswald was shot and killed by a private citizen named Jack Ruby. Oswald's murder was captured on national television.

A Shaken Nation

The Kennedy assassination and the murder of Oswald stunned the nation. Many Americans thought guns were too easy to obtain. They called for stricter laws to restrict the sale of firearms. Several gun control bills were introduced in Congress within a week of the Kennedy assassination. None of them passed. However, a number of states and cities passed new antigun laws in the mid-1960s.

In 1968, civil rights leader Martin Luther King Jr. and Democratic presidential candidate Robert F. Kennedy were assassinated by lone gunmen, within two months of each other. The public had had enough. It demanded better control over guns. Congress quickly passed the

Martin Luther King Jr.'s 1963 March on Washington for Jobs and Freedom attracted a crowd of more than 200,000 people.

Robert F. Kennedy was killed by a gunman less than five years after his brother, President John F. Kennedy, suffered the same fate.

Gun Control Act of 1968, which replaced the Federal Firearms Act of 1938. It was the most comprehensive gun control bill to date. The act required all gun dealers to keep records of customers. It also placed stronger restrictions on the selling of guns across state and international borders. The act ended all sales of guns by mail and prohibited the sale of guns to felons, the mentally ill, and anyone under the age of 18. It was praised by gun control activists. However, pro-gun groups such as the NRA portrayed it as a direct attack on Americans' right to bear arms.

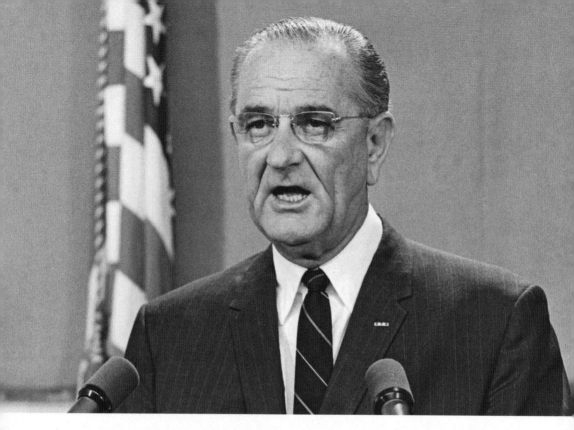

President Lyndon B. Johnson (above) asked Congress to enact stronger gun control laws after the shootings of Martin Luther King Jr. and Robert F. Kennedy.

Rise of the NRA

The NRA was once a small organization promoting gun safety and marksmanship. By the 1960s, it had grown into a powerful national group that stood against gun

A FIRSTHAND LOOK AT
THE GUN CONTROL ACT OF 1968

The Gun Control Act of 1968 was passed in response to the assassinations of Martin Luther King Jr. and Robert F. Kennedy. Its stronger gun control laws helped reignite the controversy over Second Amendment rights. See page 60 for a link to read the act online.

control laws. By 1978, the NRA had more than one million paying members. It had 300 employees and a headquarters in Washington, D.C.

The NRA created the Institute for Legislative Action, a subgroup responsible for **lobbying** against gun control in Congress. By the mid-1970s, one-quarter of the NRA's $16.5 million budget went toward lobbying activities. Its arguments against gun control were built on the beliefs that such laws proved ineffective, did not reduce crime, and only made it harder for law-abiding citizens to purchase guns.

Today, NRA lobbyists such as Jeff Freeman (left) often meet with lawmakers and attempt to gain their support in fighting gun control laws.

The Brady Bill

On March 30, 1981, President Ronald Reagan was leaving a Washington, D.C., hotel when 25-year-old John Hinckley Jr. fired six bullets at him from close range. The president and three other people were hit. Reagan recovered from his chest wound. His press secretary, James Brady, was not so lucky. Brady was wounded in the head. He suffered permanent brain damage and partial paralysis. Brady and his wife, Sarah, became major gun control activists.

Secret Service agents scrambled to gain control of the situation after President Ronald Reagan was shot in March 1981.

In 1987, they proposed the Brady Handgun Violence Prevention Act, also known as the Brady Bill. The bill called for a seven-day waiting period before anyone could purchase a gun. During this time, police could run a thorough background check to assure the buyer wasn't a criminal or mentally ill. The bill also called for the creation of a national computerized background check system to make this process easier. The NRA lobbied heavily to ensure that Congress would not approve the bill. For the next several years, the Brady Bill was presented and voted down by Congress each year.

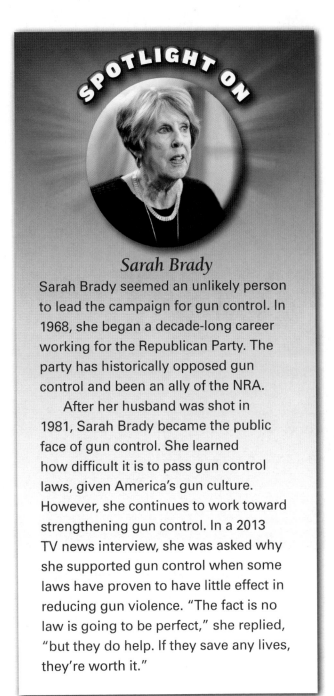

SPOTLIGHT ON

Sarah Brady

Sarah Brady seemed an unlikely person to lead the campaign for gun control. In 1968, she began a decade-long career working for the Republican Party. The party has historically opposed gun control and been an ally of the NRA.

After her husband was shot in 1981, Sarah Brady became the public face of gun control. She learned how difficult it is to pass gun control laws, given America's gun culture. However, she continues to work toward strengthening gun control. In a 2013 TV news interview, she was asked why she supported gun control when some laws have proven to have little effect in reducing gun violence. "The fact is no law is going to be perfect," she replied, "but they do help. If they save any lives, they're worth it."

James (seated right) and Sarah Brady (second from right) were at President Bill Clinton's side as he signed the Brady Bill into law.

Finally, in 1993, Congress passed the bill, and it was signed into law by President Bill Clinton. During congressional negotiations, the waiting period for a gun purchase was reduced to five days. However, the bill was still seen as a triumph for the Bradys and their supporters.

The Firearms Owners' Protection Act

Meanwhile, gun control opponents saw a victory in 1986 when they helped pass the Firearms Owners' Protection Act. This law reversed some of the rules of the Gun Control Act of 1968. Gun dealers no longer had to keep records of ammunition sales. The law allowed rifles and shotguns to be sold across state lines and made it easier for private citizens to sell and buy guns. It also called for additional penalties for criminals using guns in robberies and other crimes.

The line between those for and against gun control was clearly drawn. In the 1990s and beyond, the struggle between these two groups continued to intensify.

A VIEW FROM ABROAD

European nations generally have far stricter gun laws than the United States. Many of these nations have long been critical of the American gun culture. This is especially true in Great Britain, which has some of the toughest gun control laws in the world. "How many gun deaths does it take for American politicians to crack down on the availability of deadly weapons?" wrote columnist Alex Slater in the British newspaper the *Guardian*. "Seemingly no number is high enough." In reaction to the failure of politicians to pass stronger gun laws, one German journalist wrote, "The reaction is always the same: shock, disbelief, sadness, prayers, repression. How can it be?"

CHAPTER 4

RAISING THE STAKES

Patrick Purdy fired at least 106 bullets from his assault rifle into a crowded schoolyard during recess.

ON JANUARY 17, 1989, 26-year-old Patrick Purdy returned to the elementary school in Stockton, California, that he had attended years earlier. Armed with an AK-47 assault rifle and a pistol, Purdy opened fire on the school playground. He killed 5 children and wounded 33 others and a teacher before shooting himself.

Family members comforted postal workers who survived a shooting at a post office in Edmond, Oklahoma, on August 20, 1986.

The Stockton shootings were not the worst mass killings by a lone gunman in the 1980s. Many more people died in shootings at a post office in Oklahoma and a McDonald's restaurant in California. What was shocking to many Americans, however, was that these victims were young children and that they had been killed with an assault rifle.

War on Assault Rifles

The public response was twofold. Many people wanted to ban the selling of assault rifles and other semiautomatic weapons. They believed such weapons had no use in hunting and sport. Others simply wanted to keep guns out of schools. President George H. W. Bush issued an executive order banning the importing of semiautomatic rifles. However, this did not ban the sale of semiautomatic rifles made in the United States.

In 1990, Congress passed the Gun-Free School Zones Act. It outlawed the possession of any firearm within 1,000 feet (305 meters) of school property. The Supreme Court later overturned the law, ruling it unconstitutional. The law was revised as the Gun-Free School Zones Act of 1995 but applied only to guns brought over states lines. It also required that any student who brings a gun to school be suspended for a year.

Signs posted at schools warn people that it is illegal to carry guns on school property.

Despite concerns over losing the right to bear arms, a majority of Americans believed something more needed to be done about assault weapons, which are designed specifically for killing people. In 1994, Congress passed the Violent Crime Control and Law Enforcement Act. The act called for a complete ban for a period of 10 years on the manufacture, sale, and possession of 19 kinds of semiautomatic weapons, including AK-47s. In addition, it required that **magazines** could not be made to hold more than 10 bullets each. The act expired in 2004 and has not been renewed.

An AK-47 assault rifle is capable of firing dozens of bullets within just a few seconds.

Mourners were overwhelmed with sadness at the tragedy of the shootings at Columbine High School in Colorado.

More Mass Shootings

The new laws did not stop two high school students, Eric Harris and Dylan Klebold, from attacking their fellow classmates at Columbine High School, in Littleton, Colorado, on April 20, 1999. Harris and Klebold used assault rifles to kill 12 students and one teacher before killing themselves. The Columbine shootings shocked the nation, and schools everywhere increased their efforts to check students for guns. In part because of lobbying by the NRA and opposition from the Republican Party, the House of Representatives voted down a bill requiring background checks for sales at gun shows, and child safety trigger locks on guns.

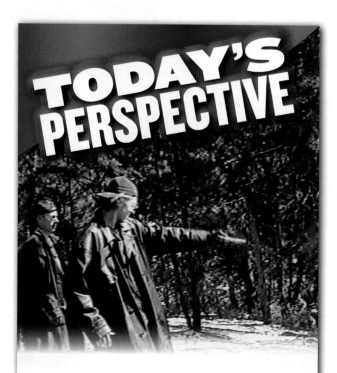

TODAY'S PERSPECTIVE

At the time of the Columbine tragedy, it was widely believed that Eric Harris (left) and Dylan Klebold (right) were seeking revenge on students who bullied them. Today it is clear from interviews with people who knew them, the diaries they kept, and other evidence that this was not the case. Harris and Klebold wanted to set off bombs at the school and kill everyone inside. When the bombs malfunctioned, the two friends turned to shooting people instead. "These are not ordinary kids who were bullied into retaliation. . . .These are kids with serious psychological problems," said psychologist Peter Langman, who has written a book on the Columbine killings.

Public opinion against uncontrolled gun ownership spiked in 2007 after 32 students were killed by a classmate at Virginia Tech, a university in Blacksburg, Virginia. It was the worst school shooting to date. Five years later, 12 people were killed in a movie theater in Aurora, Colorado, at a midnight showing of a Batman movie. But it was only after the December 14, 2012, shooting massacre at Sandy Hook Elementary School in Newtown, Connecticut, that the nation seemed ready to enforce stronger gun control laws.

A national tragedy, the Newtown shooting

A FIRSTHAND LOOK AT
PRESIDENT OBAMA'S
SPEECH AT NEWTOWN

On December 16, 2012, President Obama visited Newtown, CT, to speak at a vigil for those killed in a school massacre. "No single law, no set of laws, can eliminate evil from the world or prevent every senseless act of violence in our society," he said. "But that can't be an excuse for inaction. Surely we can do better than this." See page 60 for a link to watch a video of the president's speech online.

gripped the country's attention for weeks. President Barack Obama spoke at a prayer vigil in Newtown and vowed to strengthen gun control laws in order to prevent such tragedies from happening in the future.

At a December 16, 2012, vigil for the victims of the Newtown shooting, President Obama was emotional as he spoke of the need for stronger gun control.

Another Defeat for Gun Control

In the months following Newtown, President Obama and leading Democratic congressional leaders put together a bill to strengthen gun control. Among the bill's supporters was former Arizona congressperson Gabrielle Giffords. On January 8, 2011, Giffords had been shot in the head in an assassination attempt that took the lives of several other people. The bill called for expanded background checks on gun buyers. It would also ban assault weapons and high-capacity gun magazines. Polls showed that a vast majority of

Since being shot in 2011, former U.S. representative Gabrielle Giffords has become one of the nation's leading supporters of stronger gun control laws.

Many Americans believe that gun control laws would violate their constitutional rights.

Americans agreed with most of the bill. The NRA and most Republicans in Congress came out against the bill. They proposed instead that armed guards be placed in every school in America to combat the violence.

When the Senate voted on the bill in April 2013, it failed to get the required number of votes. The bill's supporters were devastated by the unexpected defeat. In a press conference, President Obama called it "a pretty shameful day for Washington." He then added, "Sooner or later, we are going to get this right. The memories of these children demand it."

As an ally of the NRA, Republican senator Ted Cruz is strongly opposed to gun control.

The senators who voted against the bill, mostly Republicans, had a different view. Texas senator Ted Cruz called the vote "a crucial victory for the Second Amendment." Senator Charles E. Grassley of Iowa reasoned, "Criminals do not submit to background checks now. . . . They will not submit to expanded background checks."

Two Different Views

Both sides of the gun control debate are sincere in their beliefs. Those opposed to stricter gun control think any additional laws against gun ownership will be an attack on the Second Amendment and the right "to keep and bear arms." Gun control supporters believe the Second Amendment is aimed at states and their militias. They believe that it doesn't grant the individual the absolute right to bear arms. They see the epidemic of gun violence and crime in America as evidence that stronger gun control is needed. They also highlight the fact that more Americans have died from gun violence since 1968 than have died in all the wars our nation has fought.

On January 21, 2013, hundreds of protesters gathered in New York City to call for stricter gun laws.

Gun control opponents point to statistics showing that gun control laws in states and cities have done little to reduce crime rates. They say that Americans need guns to protect their families and property when the police can't be there to protect them. Gun control supporters point to statistics showing that homes with guns are nearly five times more likely to be the scene of a suicide or nearly three times more likely to be the scene of a murder than homes without guns.

James Porter (right) is the current president of the NRA.

James W. Porter II

Gun control opponents also believe that if a restriction is put on one kind of gun, it will eventually lead to citizens losing the right to possess any firearms. "[T]here will never be a time when strident voices among our opponents will not be after our last six-shooter, then our rifle, then our shotgun," said Harlon B. Carter, a former executive vice president of the NRA. However, most gun control supporters insist that they have no intention of taking away weapons used for hunting and other shooting sports.

One thing is certain—both sides are passionate and have no intention of giving up on the issue of gun control.

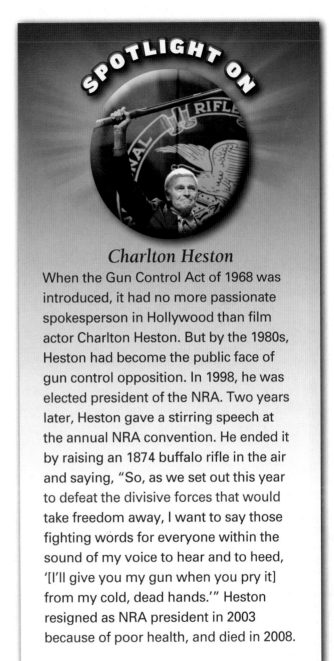

SPOTLIGHT ON

Charlton Heston

When the Gun Control Act of 1968 was introduced, it had no more passionate spokesperson in Hollywood than film actor Charlton Heston. But by the 1980s, Heston had become the public face of gun control opposition. In 1998, he was elected president of the NRA. Two years later, Heston gave a stirring speech at the annual NRA convention. He ended it by raising an 1874 buffalo rifle in the air and saying, "So, as we set out this year to defeat the divisive forces that would take freedom away, I want to say those fighting words for everyone within the sound of my voice to hear and to heed, '[I'll give you my gun when you pry it] from my cold, dead hands.'" Heston resigned as NRA president in 2003 because of poor health, and died in 2008.

What Happened Where?

OREGON

IDAHO

NORTH DAKOTA

SOUTH DAKOTA

WYOMING

NEVADA

UTAH

Littleton ●

COLORADO

NEBRASKA

CALIFORNIA

KANSAS

ARIZONA

NEW MEXICO

OKLAHOMA

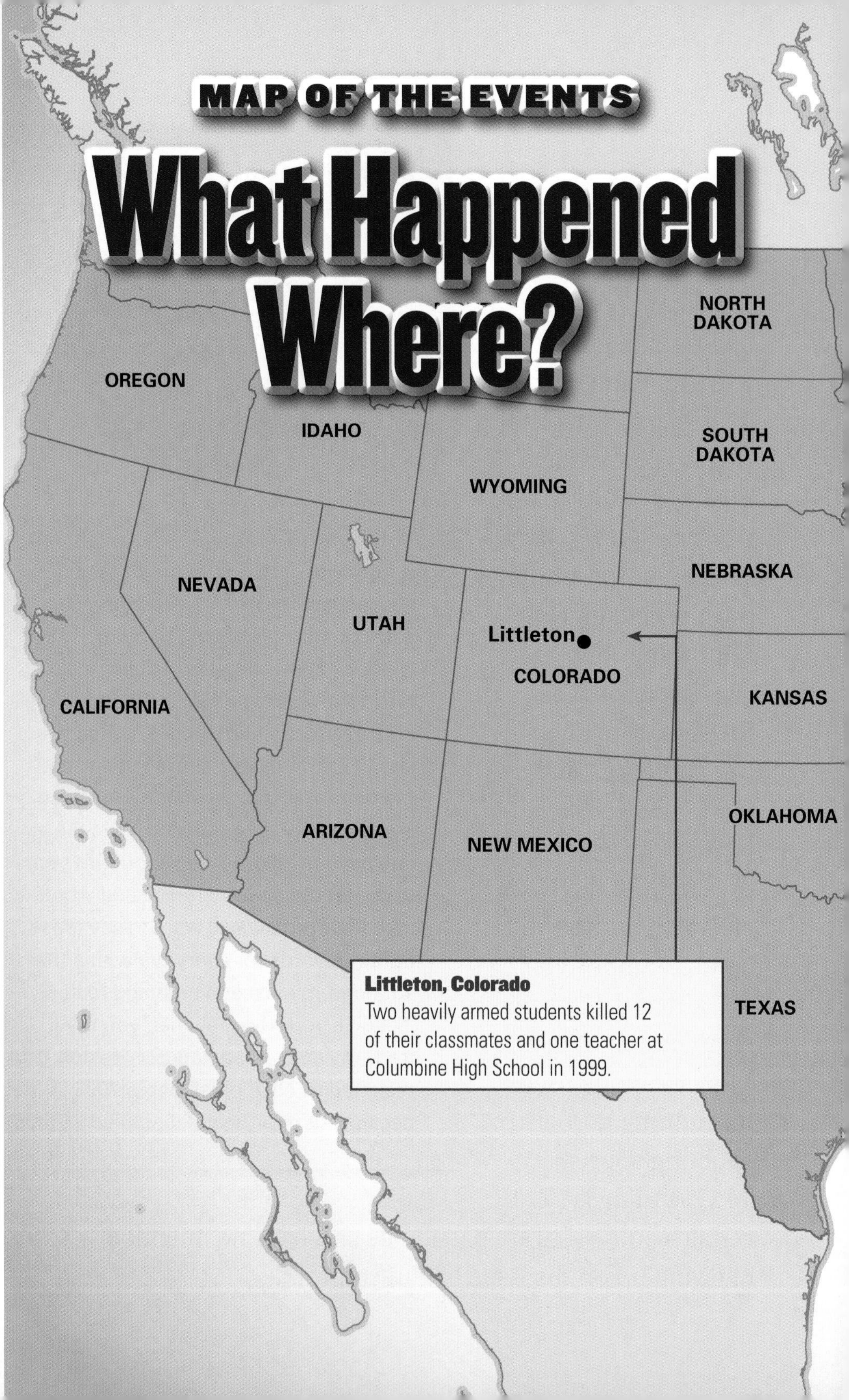

Littleton, Colorado
Two heavily armed students killed 12 of their classmates and one teacher at Columbine High School in 1999.

TEXAS

Newtown, Connecticut
Lone gunman Adam Lanza killed 26 people as well as himself at an elementary school on December 14, 2012.

Lexington and Concord, Massachusetts
The first battles of the American Revolution were fought here between British troops and colonial militiamen in April 1775.

MINNESOTA

VERMONT

MAINE

NH

WISCONSIN

Concord Lexington
MA

MICHIGAN

NEW YORK
Newtown

RI

CT

IOWA

PENNSYLVANIA
Philadelphia

NEW JERSEY

OHIO

DELAWARE

ILLINOIS INDIANA

Washington, D.C. ✪

MARYLAND

WEST
VIRGINIA

MISSOURI

VIRGINIA

KENTUCKY

NORTH
CAROLINA

TENNESSEE

ARKANSAS

SOUTH
CAROLINA

MISSISSIPPI

GEORGIA

Philadelphia, Pennsylvania
James Madison and other state representatives created the Bill of Rights, including the Second Amendment, in 1790.

ALABAMA

LOUISIANA

N
W E
S

0   100   200 mi

0   100   200 km

FLORIDA

Washington, D.C.
Congress has passed a number of federal gun control laws throughout history. However, on April 17, 2013, it voted down a bill proposed after the Newtown, Connecticut, massacre.

THE STORY CONTINUES

Rights vs. Safety

Many Americans enjoy shooting targets at gun ranges.

The issue of gun control will continue to be argued and debated by fair-minded Americans for years to come. In the United States, guns no longer play the central role in survival that they once did. Yet many Americans believe that the right to own and use guns is a freedom that shouldn't be taken away.

ALMOST 17 MILLION AMERICANS

People call for better gun control laws in the aftermath of terrible gun violence, but their enthusiasm often disappears over time. The right of gun owners to keep their guns could be balanced with the rights of citizens to be free from fear and violence. While there are extremists on both sides, most Americans fall somewhere in the middle. They want to find a way to keep guns away from criminals and the mentally disturbed, while allowing law-abiding citizens to purchase and own them. They may support some gun control, such as background checks and a ban on assault or semiautomatic firearms, but oppose other restrictions. Until both sides of the issue of gun control are willing to compromise and meet each other halfway, it is unlikely this pressing social issue will be resolved.

Guns can be useful tools when they are used responsibly.

APPLIED TO PURCHASE GUNS IN 2012.

INFLUENTIAL INDIVIDUALS

Charlton Heston

Sarah Brady

James Madison (1751–1836) was one of the main authors of the U.S. Constitution and the main writer of the Bill of Rights. He later became the fourth president of the United States, serving from 1809 to 1817.

Charlton Heston (1923–2008) was a film actor who served as president of the National Rifle Association from 1998 to 2003.

Sarah Brady (1942–) is a leading spokesperson for gun control. With her husband, James Brady, she was coauthor of the Brady Bill, an important gun law that was passed in 1993.

Barack Obama (1961–), the 44th president of the United States, has made gun control an important issue in the second term of his presidency.

Adam Lanza (1992–2012) was the gunman who shot and killed his mother and then 26 students, teachers, and administrators at Sandy Hook Elementary School in Newtown, Connecticut. It was the second-worst school massacre to date in U.S. history.

Barack Obama

TIMELINE

1791

December
The Bill of Rights becomes part of the U.S. Constitution and includes the Second Amendment, which addresses the right to keep and bear arms.

1871

The National Rifle Association (NRA) is founded by two Civil War veterans.

1963

November 22
President John F. Kennedy is assassinated by a lone gunman, Lee Harvey Oswald, in Dallas, Texas.

November 24
Lee Harvey Oswald is killed by a citizen, Jack Ruby.

1968

The Gun Control Act becomes law, replacing the Federal Firearms Act of 1938.

1927

The Miller Act, the first federal gun control law, is passed by Congress and makes mailing guns through the U.S. postal system illegal.

1934

The National Firearms Act, the first comprehensive gun control law, is passed.

1938

The Federal Firearms Act requires gun manufacturers and sellers to get a license to ship guns out of state.

1993

After several years of being voted down by Congress, the Brady Bill passes.

1999

April 20
Two heavily armed teenagers kill 13 people at Columbine High School in Littleton, Colorado, before killing themselves.

2012

December 14
A 20-year-old gunman shoots and kills 26 people and then himself at Sandy Hook Elementary School in Newtown, Connecticut.

2013

April 17
The U.S. Senate votes down a comprehensive gun control bill supported by President Obama.

LIVING HISTORY

Primary sources provide firsthand evidence about a topic. Witnesses to a historical event create primary sources. They include autobiographies, newspaper reports of the time, oral histories, photographs, and memoirs. A secondary source analyzes primary sources, and is one step or more removed from the event. Secondary sources include textbooks, encyclopedias, and commentaries. To view the following primary and secondary sources, go to www.factsfornow.scholastic.com. Enter the keywords **Gun Control** and look for the Living History logo ∑.

∑ The Federal Firearms Act of 1938 The Federal Firearms Act was a major piece of gun control legislation signed by President Franklin D. Roosevelt on June 30, 1938. It required gun sellers to obtain a license for shipping guns across state lines.

∑ The Gun Control Act of 1968 The Gun Control Act of 1968 required all gun dealers to keep records of customers, placed stronger restrictions on the selling of guns across state and international borders, and ended all sales of guns by mail. It also prohibited the sale of guns to felons, the mentally ill, and anyone under the age of 18.

∑ President Obama's Speech at Newtown The 2012 massacre at Sandy Hook Elementary School in Newtown, Connecticut, was a turning point for the gun control debate and the Obama administration. On December 16, 2012, at a vigil for the victims, President Obama spoke about the need for stricter gun control.

∑ The Virginia Declaration of Rights The Virginia Declaration of Rights was one of James Madison's inspirations for the wording of the Second Amendment. It states, "That a well-regulated militia, composed of the body of the people, trained to arms, is the proper, natural, and safe defense of a free state."

RESOURCES

Books

Harrison, Geoffrey, and Thomas F. Scott. *Lethal Weapons*. Chicago: Norwood House Press, 2013.

MacKay, Jenny. *Gun Control*. Detroit: Lucent Books, 2013.

Nakaya, Andrea C. *Gun Control and Violence*. San Diego, CA: ReferencePoint Press, 2014.

Scherer, Lauri S., ed. *Gun Violence*. Detroit: Greenhaven Press, 2013.

Valdez, Angela, and John E. Ferguson Jr. *Gun Control*. New York: Chelsea House, 2011.

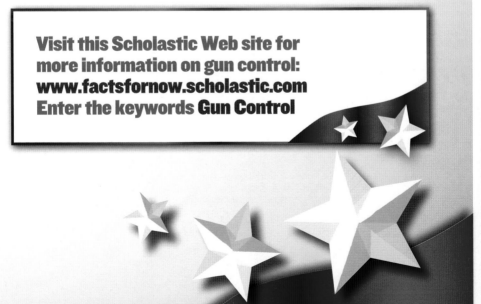

Visit this Scholastic Web site for more information on gun control: www.factsfornow.scholastic.com Enter the keywords Gun Control

GLOSSARY

amendments (uh-MEND-muhnts) changes that are made to a law or legal document

anarchist (AN-ar-kust) a person who believes that government is not necessary

arsenals (AR-suh-nuhlz) places where weapons and ammunition are stored

constitution (kahn-stuh-TOO-shuhn) the basic laws of a country that state the rights of the people and the powers of the government

felons (FEL-uhnz) people who have committed serious crimes, such as murder or burglary

lobbying (LAH-bee-ing) working to influence politicians on specific issues

magazines (MAG-uh-zeenz) the parts of guns that hold bullets

militias (muh-LISH-uhz) groups of people who are trained to fight but who aren't professional soldiers

muskets (MUHS-kits) long guns that were used by soldiers before the rifle was invented

semiautomatic (seh-mee-aw-tuh-MAT-ik) capable of firing a bullet every time the trigger is pulled without needing to be reloaded or cocked

Page numbers in *italics* indicate illustrations.

ABOUT THE AUTHOR

Steven Otfinoski has written more than 150 books for young readers. Three of his nonfiction books have been chosen Books for the Teen Age by the New York Public Library. Among his Scholastic books are the best-selling *Putting It In Writing* and *The Kid's Guide to Money*. Otfinoski lives in Connecticut with his wife, an English teacher, their daughter, and two dogs.